A
Caring Man's
View in

Poetry

GARY MARK WAYNE GAAL

BALBOA.
PRESS

A DIVISION OF HAY HOUSE

Balboa Press books may be ordered through booksellers or by contacting:

Balboa Press
A Division of Hay House
1663 Liberty Drive
Bloomington, IN 47403
www.balboapress.com.au
1 (877) 407-4847

Because of the dynamic nature of the Internet, any web addresses or links contained in this book may have changed since publication and may no longer be valid. The views expressed in this work are solely those of the author and do not necessarily reflect the views of the publisher, and the publisher hereby disclaims any responsibility for them.

The author of this book does not dispense medical advice or prescribe the use of any technique as a form of treatment for physical, emotional, or medical problems without the advice of a physician, either directly or indirectly. The intent of the author is only to offer information of a general nature to help you in your quest for emotional and spiritual well-being. In the event you use any of the information in this book for yourself, which is your constitutional right, the author and the publisher assume no responsibility for your actions.

Any people depicted in stock imagery provided by Thinkstock are models, and such images are being used for illustrative purposes only. Certain stock imagery © Thinkstock.

Print information available on the last page.

ISBN: 978-1-5043-1077-2 (sc)
ISBN: 978-1-5043-1078-9 (e)

Balboa Press rev. date: 10/20/2017

Acknowledgements

I would like to thank my sister Sandra Gaal Hayman for sharing her insights and offering her time and efforts to my book.

Also thanks to Balboa Press.

Foreword

In 1988 my brother Gary Mark Wayne Gaal penned 47 poems in 47 consecutive days. Gary has not written anything since. Inspiration is often something mysterious its origins we do not always understand.

When Gary was young he was involved in the Scout Movement before joining the Australian Defence Force when aged 17 years.

He also enjoyed participating in many sporting activities and excelled in this area.

Due to medical circumstances after 3 years of service he was discharged in 1979. The impact of his discharge was devastating, as serving his country was all Gary wanted to do in life, having a strong family history of those who served their country.

Not long after his discharge Gary suffered a Manic Depressive (Bipolar) episode triggered by the stress and disappointment at his ended career. What followed was many years of psychiatric inpatient and outpatient care and a journey into mental illness. There were periods of isolation, lost self-esteem and friends who left his life at this critical time.

After overcoming many setbacks, Gary is ready to share his poetic insights. I hope as you read and enjoy this collection of poems aptly titled "A Caring Man's View in Poetry" you will come to see the heart and soul of my brother Gary (Gunner) Gaal, the sensitive man he is and the empathy he feels for others despite the life-changing situations he has faced.

Sandra Gaal Hayman

Love And Peace

I can see your face still
Even though you're not there
You taught me to believe
It's love we need to share
Through hope we can achieve
A peace in our hearts
A place to learn to give
Love from the start
So why must it be?
The child crying out
The world refuses to see
What the hunger's all about
But there is starting
A new light on the horizon
Shining down on me
A new page in our history
The story of you and me
Just take the time to listen
To listen to its song
A voice of love and peace
So the world can get along.

Cry Again

Who needs a reason to cry?
A man will cry alone, silent
A woman will share
But the child cries only
For a good reason
As the baby born
Takes its first breath of life
Unprotected, unashamed
Unafraid to shed a tear
That's the unteachable emotion of all
But as we grow up
How many forget?
How many must learn to cry again?
How about it, will you try?
To learn again to cry.

Don't Fret Sister

Well hi, top of the morning
New day a dawning
Look up, sun shining on me
What's that I hear, high up in the tree?
A little bird singing
His song here for me
Singing, no need to panic
No need to cry
Just look up
Look me in the eye
Saying don't worry brother
Say here's my hand
Don't fret sister
I'll be here to understand.

Family Of Man

I'm not one to be accomplished
Not one needing to pass the tests
But at least I sit down
To try them, to give it all my best
To know I gave myself
That chance to learn something new
To be able to openly relate
How great a way to view,
To learn to live a life
Look at the grown tree with its strong roots
It always needs water
To nourish it along
We need that too to live
Our seeds for the future
Has to be planted first
But it takes love and understanding
For our roots to grow strong in an adult tree
Then the fruits of knowledge
Can be harvested then stored successfully
So the blessing is shared between
The entire family of man.

Here For Me

The rain comes and it goes
Sometimes hail, sometimes snow
Still it beats in my heart
Always there from the start
Can you listen to it fall
Does it answer to my call?
To quench the world of its thirst
Asking only where to land first
On the trees, on the grass
It will come to pass
I'm afraid of the day
When no rain comes
Anyway, no sun in the sky
No earth in my eye
I'm afraid this will be
The end of it all here for me.

I Saw A Tear

I saw a tear in your eye
Never asked you why
Never knew you could cry
You never did before
I didn't know what to do
Except to say I love you
But to reach out my hand
To offer, to understand
That this was new to you
That you were feeling blue
I needed to show I care
At last now it was something
That we now share.

Looking Through A Child's Eyes

Looking through a child's eyes
Seeing things around
Noticing the confusion that abounds
Trusting the young, trusting the old
Trusting the stories, that they are told
What we are, they are
What we do, they do
What we say, they say
So people choose yourself
How about you?
Don't label a person's view
Don't criticise
People tend to judge
But don't analyse
Asking the questions
To learn what you can
I would direct them to a child
Then to pay a qualified man.

Memo To A Friend

Life is a journey
With a beginning and an end
I'd like to write this poem to you
Memo to a friend
I knew you for a moment
It just seems like years
But in that brief encounter
We shared laughter and tears
Your faith was so simple
Principles were clear
You said trust one another
Love without fear
Listen to people
To learn what you can
From the young child
Up to the old man
For their eyes see the stories
Their words tell the tales
Like that ship of the desert
No wind in its sails
So let's grow into flowers
Not into weeds
Always remember friendship
Starts with the seeds
Yes, life is that journey
With its beginning and its end
I wish to end this poem for you
A dedication to my friend.

My Dreams

My dreams they say
Hey face reality
For my hope is in my dream
For the children to be
What people say
I don't give a damn
Putting labels on
Lord knows who I am
But their words they hurt me
They cut like a knife
From the people who don't know me
Family, acquaintances and like
I walk away again
Thinking there I could find a friend
Bitten once more
Lonely again.

Our Time Is Now

In the land of no horizons
Where no wind ever stirs
People who without faces
People who are never heard
Standing up for what they believe in
Who have listened and then found
Have found the trumpet note of freedom
Is such a sweet sound
Today the myth of the past
Which everyone thinks is still there
Is coming back to haunt us
Now we're seeing how they cared
How they lived and died
Were respected and honoured
Where a man's view was accepted
Today we're labelled not as originals
But as sheep to follow
A man stands up today
Straight away rejected
You may listen to me
You may walk away
But when we do speak
Into each other's eyes
Our time is now
Contact is there
Communication is not dead
We must learn and practice it
Simple as it seems to be
Common sense know how
Between you and me.

Someone Who Cares

If only there was someone
To listen when I was feeling down and out
Someone to take the time to listen
I thought what is it all about?
Instead you turn away
From what I have to say
Like a tooth with an ache
No wonder eventually I did break
Then they fed me full of drugs
To make me see their reality
Three times a day
They tried to change my personality
Never again, that was the end
Never took drugs again
Then the patients who were there
Only they in the world seemed to care
They listened to my story
And I to theirs
It seemed so sad that only they
And it was there that
I found finally
Someone who cares.

Teachers Of The Mind

A vision of the song came to mind
My own song, my own mind
Written down, empty pages of time
Not recorded, no specific kind
Children of today, no-one to guide
Go their own way, their eyes are blind
A reason for this, a need to find
Teachers of the mind
To show young how to fly
On life's journeys, we need a guide.

Tell Me

Tell me old man
What your eyes have seen
Help me know
Help me learn to live
Show me, old man
What love really means
Today accepting others
Is not what it seems
Tell me, young man
Do you like what you see?
Conflicts and war
Prejudice and poverty
Help me understand
Why this must be so?
I want to live in peace
In a world where peace can grow
Listen, old man
I want to know
What's in your heart?
Tell me please
Your story from the start
The hurt of your past
Is just in your way
I want to learn about how you feel now
And how you felt yesterday.

The Other Side Of Life

Hear the beat of the drum
Our life has just begun
The past is just a memory
Now there's only you and me
To laugh
To sing
To experience everything
Joy in our hearts
Here's where it starts
Let's have a girl or boy
A bundle of joy
To love
To teach
To guide
To the other side of life.

The Rain Weeps

The rain weeps from the cloud
Hungry people crying out loud
Thunder claps from the bombs
Lightning flash, what went wrong
With the world, with the peace
We must negotiate a new lease
Strike up a master plan
A new hope, a new land
Where there's no conflicts
Only peace, no rejection
Hatred ceased
No criticism or need to judge
People's motives and lives
Trusting others
Must survive
To see nothing
But smiles everywhere
Nothing to hurt
No despair
If you feel like I do
Take a step, voice your view
No need to start up a great band
Just pass this onto someone
Who will understand?

The Spirit Moved Me

The spirit moved me
To greater things
I am His subject
He is my King
I walk for miles Lord
Feet ached with pain
You lift me up Lord
To start again
He sent His message
To touch our lives
His praises ring out
And will survive
I sing His praises
Far and wide
The truth is living
The words alive
There are mountains
Still left to climb
Rivers there to baptize
Streams still left to ford
We are all children
Of the Lord.

Wilderness

Picture yourself
A creature high
Soaring in the wind
High up in the sky
Coming to earth
Only to feed
On plenty of plants
With plenty of leaves
See the deserts
And the wilderness
See the plants
You'd think there would be less
They're alive today
Cause we left them alone
No human takeover
To build his home
Let's protect our parks
And rainforests too
Protect the right
To protect the view
Yet we kill this land
Till nothing exists
Unless we stop
Unless we resist
We must leave it alone
For if we don't would
You want the world
To be deserts and wilderness.

Wasting My Time

Co-operation, no confrontation
Why don't we start today?
Communicating, no hesitation
Let's sit down and work out a way
No-one is listening
It's like we've forgotten how
Like people swearing
No-one caring
To try and change now
Their view is me
Never us, never we
Saying I'm number one
Never two or three
So still am I wasting my time?
Putting down these lines
Sooner or later I'll know
If I'm wasting my time.

The Light In Their Eyes

Staring at the ceiling
The light in my eye
It attracts the insects
As they wing by and by
I'm thinking of some questions
Trying to find the answers to
Now writing them down on paper
You answer false or true
Who's going to remember the past?
Who wishes to remember the old?
Who cares to listen to their stories?
That they now only hold
The forgotten last generation
Who were once like you and me
Who did the same types of learning
Rejected by the same powers to be
Today I see the old man
The youth of today don't give a damn
To listen and learn about his life
How he corrected his mistakes
That way we might survive
He is only old, all alone
Most folks shut away
In their old folk home
What a shameful waste
Staring at the ceiling
The light in their eyes
Sad and lonely
Asking themselves, why?

The Old Man

I met an old man the other day
My friends laughed
Didn't care what he had to say
His face was worn
From experience of the past
I sat down to listen
I didn't laugh
He said son, your life has just begun
It's like a ladder
And you're on the first rung
Just by you listening
I know you care
You've learned the great lesson
Now you must be aware
Two types of people
Go hand in hand
One talks, the other listens
But who's in command?
Learn from what you hear
Draw your conclusions
Accept others views
But not their delusions
The most important thing is listening
Yes, life is the deck
And you're just one card
Learning the greatest lesson of all
People find it's so simple, it's hard.

The Game Of Listening

Hey, have you got a view?
Have you got the time?
To sit down and listen
While I speak my mind
Just look around the world
The conflict that is there
The anger and the hurt
Hunger and despair
The freedoms which are gone
Senseless killing that is wrong
A terrible sham I feel
Seeing poverty that countries deal
Building arsenals, promoting death
Instead of seeing children that are left
In a world without peace
All conflict must cease
Learning to accept
Instead of reject
People different
We've just met
That's something we neglect
Instead of saying I know you
Why don't we listen to their view?
Passing judgements of what's said
How can you know what's in my head?
Can't you accept?
Everyone's view is different
No-one is the same
So losing conversation
Now who is to blame?

Our need to communicate is based
On one thing
The easiest game on earth
The game of listening.

Grandad

Grandad was old but young in his views
He lived his life paying all of his dues
When I was younger
Living in my youth
We always talked together
Looking for the truth
He said son when my Dad talked to me
We went for a walk, he shared a joke
That made me laugh
Then I listened as he talked
He said son look around
Step sure on the ground
Don't stop don't shuffle your feet
Love what you do, and do it well
And smile at who you meet
I joined the army straight from school
Made new mates lived by the rules
Three years passed keeping my ears open
They pensioned me off
I thought they must be joking
Then I met a girl at the picture show
We fell in love, married
Don't you know?
Had a baby that grew into a boy
Then the day came
He began asking questions to me
I remembered my grandad's
Answer to my plea
We went for a walk, I shared a joke
That made him laugh

Then he listened as I talked
I said, son look around
Step sure on the ground
Don't stop, don't shuffle your feet
Love what you do
And do it well
And smile at who you meet.

History Is There

They say the old are wise
In thinking with problems they have solved
But different generations
They don't listen
They just don't listen to the old
Instead they suffer from the wrongs
That life has thrown to them
Society breaking apart
Breaking apart again
We need to build it all up
The answers in the past
The history is there
History is there
We can learn by reading about it
Seeing how they cared
It's such an easy task
Before we get too old
How about we ask
Before it's too late
Before the cycle goes round
Before long the old won't be around.

I Still Care

When all the world
Was green and simple
Where time and life
Were slowed, no rush
No need to panic
Where kids ran free to grow
Guided by adults
Having values, principles too
Passing down through families
Accepting each other's view
Where young and old had choices
Freedom and happiness
Support and instruction
Discipline to self- determine
To choose right from young
To be shown good from evil
Through practical common sense
Application of life
I ask where the principles are now
Tell me if you dare
Hey, I'm still listening
I still care.

Looking For A Friend

I'm looking for a friend
Seeing no-one there
I'm looking for a friend
Someone to care
Searching for a smile
Someone to listen for awhile
Nobody there, no-one will care
About peace in the world
The boy and the girl
Hungry and sad
Is this the way we're going to leave it?
Dying young, their life just begun
Their lives are misery
Is this the way we're going to leave it?
Black and white yellow and brown
Each body bleeds red
Can you see the difference?
Capital gains
No aches or pains
Majority rules
Is this the way we're going to leave it?
Everybody searching
For the smiles
Nothing is there
No-one to care, mankind doesn't care
Is this the way we're going to leave it?

That Was Me Yesterday

Laying on my bed
Feeling depressed
Thoughts and fantasies
Floating to the ceiling
Thinking of people
Who have suppressed
My emotions and ideas
And what I believe in
Now I look through the window
The sky is blue
I see in the window visions of you
The tree blowing in the wind
The children at play
The one with the dog
That was me yesterday.

From The Outside

Looking in from the outside
What can you see?
People searching for a book
In the library
Most just see the titles
And bypass on to the next
But the person who will open seeing its theme
To discover original views
We are all unique and individual
How many people in the world
Everyone has a different story
Memories of life
We never stop learning
Until we die
Can't you see how simple it would be?
To give everyone time to tell their story
We must be prepared to listen
First to take a seat in today's society
Do we all have freedom of speech?
How about freedom to listen
To think, to laugh, to talk
To smile, to love
I hope we can all have this everywhere today
But do you have a choice?
Well, do you?

How About You

I'm free like the eagle in the wind
Like the birds who love to sing
I'm the sun who wants to shine
A free spirit who loves mankind
One spark who wants to ignite
Families, countries, hey stop the fight
Let's all listen to what I say
Maybe we can start today
People next to you
Whether black, white or blue
Turn around and smile
Take time out for awhile
Then put out your hand
Whether you're a woman, a child or a man
Say how you are
Smile as you say this too
How are you?
What a way to make a friend
If we can bottle this again
Package it express, then mail it to the U.N
Maybe then they'll see
A friend in you and me
Pass the bottle round
Everyone share the drink
Peace, justice and the right to think
Here's my glass, I'm thirsty too
How about you?

I Wish For You

Blue skies around the sun
New day just begun
Old songs to be sung
That's what I give to you
Young hearts need to feel
Someone who is real
It's not a great deal
That's what I say to you
Come on and laugh
Come on and cry
Come take a seat
Before you die
Come on and smile
You only live for awhile
Take the time to give
Take the time to live
Come touch a life
Reach out, take my hand
Even though you don't understand
Just trust your fellow man
That's what I leave to you
Don't waste a chance today
Three words that are hard to say
To say-
I love you
Old friends are gone again
New friends to make amends
I wish this never ends
That's what I wish for you.

Why Do I Cry

Why do I cry?
When the movie is over
Why do I weep?
Seeing the story unfold
Why wipe the tears?
That swell up inside me
It doesn't matter
If anyone sees
Why don't you cry?
When children are dying
Why don't you weep?
Seeing the never ending story
You can't see their tears
That swell up inside them
It does matter
If everyone's blind.

Yesterday's Clown

Yesterday's clown
But he smiles no more
No-one around
To knock at his door
Thinking back
How he'd love to rearrange
Yesterday's dreams
But he dreams no more
He thought he lost reality
His dreams coming true
Just wasn't to be
Gone again, still lives in the past
Searching for friends that didn't last
Yesterday's clown
But he laughs no more
Yesterday's dreams
Walk out the door
The past is buried
And dead they say
Then he'll ask
Who'll show him the way?
Back to the past
Back to the loves
Back to life.

Suddenly

Common bonds bring people together
Togetherness is what we need to share
Happiness is waiting there for you and me
Only love will be
Suddenly I see
I was blind no need to see again
I was lost looking for a friend
Then I saw for the first time in my life
Someone was real
Suddenly I feel
I'm alive for the first time in my life
Got to sing, sing out far and wide
There's a place waiting for you
Inside come take my heart
It's just a start-
Take my life, it's yours to command
Take my soul I put it in your hands
I'm alive for the first time in my life
Suddenly I feel someone is real
In my heart, in my soul, in my life.

Moonrise Sunrise

Moonrise, sunrise
A day must begin
To give peace and harmony
So hunger can't win
To hear children's laughter
To see faces smile
What are societies after?
When you give an inch- they take a mile
How can we change this?
I ask myself eagerly
What is the world after?
New values do exist
To change the system
People have to say no and resist.

Across The Sea

Across the sea
Tell you what I saw
No more war
In the sky
What did I spy?
Sun shining on me
On the earth
What did I see?
No poverty that's for me
Tracks in the sand
Where are they leading to?
Follow that step
Into the world
Peace everywhere
If you've got a care
His message recorded fact
Follow that
Time to follow him
Jump in, take a swim
Step in to the morning
Rhythm in my feet
Sounds of the world
Stepping to the beat
Smile at the people
Everywhere you go
Just seeing you friendly
Is what they need to know?

Clear My Mind

I had a dream
A dream journey to the future
Where roads never end
But join together forever
Seeing the old man guide the boy
Who asks for answers instead of toys?
One spirit looking back
To others seeking, to know
I wish this wasn't a dream
I wish this could be so
Memories of the past
Still flood my mind
Turning thoughts into words
Freeing scars of time
To free my mind
I had a thought
A thought to bring
People together
Not just for a day
But until the end of time
Where everyone learns to love
Give up hate, no push, no shove
This thought is what I feel
I wish it could be real
Memories of my past
Still haunt my mind
Turning thoughts into words
Freeing the scars of time
Clearing up my mind
To clear my mind.

Common Bonds

I wonder why the Prime Minister
Goes around proclaiming
To go into bat for the common man
How can any politician or
Anybody relate to a job
To expire an opinion if
Never going through a similar
Experience in a society
Being led by no common bonds
Is it remiss of me to ask?
Where is the honest man today?
Who is to give a grass root example?
Why are we never given
A straight answer to
An inquiring question?
Why is it always lost in
Verbal rhetoric?
Is it a case of they can't give it?
If it's not shown basic concern.

Eagles In The Sky

Planes fly high
Eagles in the in sky
I care not for what they see
Looking down on a world rushing about
Most living in poverty
I care not for the man
All that scam
And the materials that they seek
But the trust of a friend
Holding out his hand
Love who needs to speak
When I have a son
I think I'll protect him
Like an eagle in his nest
Looking clear at the world
The good and the bad
Cities to the wilderness
But as he learns to spread his wings
Learning ABCs love and other things
Don't forget to let him fly
Watching and listening
In this place I pray
To the Lord for the human race
I hope one day to see
No more prejudice war or poverty
Seeing a hopeful smile
On a child's face
Helping hands filled with grace
I hope one day to see.

Leading The Blind

Education today is not of old
Where the slant was on the three R's
Personally taught by teachers
Mature in years in life's experience
Today alas secondary students are taught
By and large by kids themselves
Is it the blind
Leading the blind?
Anybody travelling
Needing a guidepost to direct them for sure
So where are the guides to teach?
The three L's for example
To look to learn, to listen
How about a teaching course
Acquire common sense or to
Teach individually or to make
Choices personally.

Sea Of Life

Into the hungry sea of life one plunges
Just like the knife
Which cut away the hurt, the fears
That seems to gather throughout the years
Then will there be a time
For love of peace, and peace of mind?
To learn to trust again
Those people who did offend
We need to make amends
Then for the hungry to be fed
For all wars
To finally end
For freedom of what is said
We need to learn to love instead.

You And Me

Times I've been mistaken
With words that I choose
People taking it wrongly
It's enough to give me the blues
To curb ones emotions
Instead of coming right out
But forever listening to some people
I wish to just stand up and shout
Yes many times I've had my ears burnt
With words that I choose
Don't sit down to listen
So which one is to lose?
It's an easy thing to wish for
Listening is an easy thing to do
But when you interrupt as usual
When you care not for my view
Hey, I'm trying just to be accepted
Remember there's always two sides
Not right or wrong
Just you and me.

In Need

You're alone again
In need
Of a friend
Your heart breaking apart
In need
Of someone to mend it
You're feeling down
No-one around
To love, to need, to share
In need
Of someone to give it
Your words never understood
Unheard never knew you could
Speak of things understood
In need
Of someone to hear it
Your praise's no-one gave
A single word
A thought your way
In need
Of someone to show it
In need.

Just Like Me

For the rest of his days
He lives in solitude
A man without cause
Nothing to lose
Barely alive, never venturing anywhere
He has no friends
Doesn't care, no hobbies
Or interests shown in events of the world
His world is his home
Hey, he looks like me
Don't you agree, just like me?
That isn't so, how do I know?
It isn't so because I know
No-one is the same
Originality has no name
Still we will put the labels on
Here's what I think
Where the world is wrong
No choices for a start
Freedom, what a farce
Only to be told what to do
Choices are made for you
Individuality has just died
Nothing to nurture, nothing to guide
How can this even be fixed?
When people and countries just can't mix
To prevent the problems
Not there, people, apathy

I don't care
I'm bringing up my son
My own way, hey yes
Don't you agree?
He looks and acts just like me.

A Friend

Laying here waiting for the sun
My old life's a mess
New life just begun
Like the water here in my glass
I'm looking crystal clear
And learning fast
To be a better man
Life is the court
And you're just a player
Wake up, take hold of it
Sooner or later
And to my friends who are highly strung
Don't smash it, don't hit and run
But take time out for me
A time to smile
A time to be fulfilled in your life
Even if you're single
Or have a wife
Regard me as a friend
Regard me as your friend.

I Am

I am what I are
I are what I do
I do what I say
My choices aren't made by you
The only person to know you
Is yourself
The only person to judge me
Is myself
The only one needed to accept this
Is me.

World And Me

Across the water to the horizon
What do I see?
Clouds silhouette in the sky
Sun peeking through at me
Across the ocean
Far and wide
What do I hear?
Great trains on the tracks
Crashing back
That's what I hear
Sitting alone watching
What do I feel?
Wishing the world would wake up
Before it's too late
With love in their hearts
Wishing that the starving eat
Wishing the wars to cease
Thinking of a time
A time of peace
Sitting here on my rock
Birds singing in the trees
A song of joy
Because he's free
No war, no poverty
Because he's free
I wish that for
The world and me.

To You My Friend

My words are here
The truth is there
Listen and learn
It's everywhere

Printed in the United States
By Bookmasters